Investing

The Definitive Beginner's Guide

Investing 101, Investment Options, 5
Crucial Mistakes To Avoid & Risk Reward
Evaluation For Rookie Investors

By Adam Richards

Table of Contents

Conclusion

Introduction

Do you ever think of how rich people make their fortunes and then keep growing it?

Do you dream of early retirement (or being able to retire at all)?

Do you always wish you could make sound investments but are confused about where to start?

This book is meant to cover the practice of investing from the basics that every beginner should know. The financial world can be quite intimidating, but I strongly believe that things will not seem as complex once you become familiar with the lingo and key concepts.

You will also learn about the building blocks and strategies that suit you best.

By the time you are done reading this book, you will be ready to invest and start enjoying your investments soon enough.

Please note that investing is not a get-rich-quick scheme. It takes work and effort, but the rewards will definitely be worth it. So do yourself a lifelong favor and keep reading.

Chapter 1:

Investing 101: The Nuts And Bolts Of Investing Simplified

What Is Investing?

Investing can be defined as the act of committing capital or money to an endeavor with the expectation of obtaining an additional income or profit.

To put it simply, investing is just putting your money where it works for you.

This is different from how most people view money. Most of us grow up being told that the only way to get rich is getting a good job and working, which is the mindset a lot of people have. However, there is a flaw with this kind of reasoning:

If you want to make more money, you have to work longer hours. Considering that there is a limit to the number of hours in a day a human being can work, there will also be a limit to the amount of income you can make from your job. Not to mention the fact that having a lot of money in the bank means absolutely nothing if you do not have the time to enjoy it.

Since you cannot clone yourself in order to increase the number of hours you work, you can choose to get your money to work on your behalf instead. This means that you can be working for your boss, sleeping, socializing, or mowing the lawn and still have your money earning more money elsewhere.

By investing, you are simply maximizing your

earning potential, regardless of whether you get a pay rise or not, work overtime or search for a better job.

Investment can be made in different ways, whether it's starting a business, investing in real estate, stocks, mutual funds or bonds. Each of these 'investment vehicles' has pros and cons, which we will discuss later in the book. The main thing to remember is that it doesn't matter which vehicle you choose; the objective is to get your money working for you and earning a profit.

Investing vs. Gambling

Do not confuse investing for gambling. Gambling is risking money by betting your money on a result that is uncertain, hoping that you will win some more money.

There might be some confusion between the two terms because some investors buy stocks due to 'hot tips', which creates a similar impression to betting in a casino.

A real investor always assesses the risks prior to making an investment. You have to do a thorough analysis and invest wisely, instead of just praying for Lady Luck to smile at you.

Fundamentals of Investing

It is true that everyone wants to have more money. In today's world, investing is becoming a necessity if you want to survive the tough turbulent times. There is simply no excuse for saying that there is not enough information out there to get you started. However, you have to keep a keen eye on the information being peddled out there. There are, of course, some fundamental principles of investing that every beginner must know. Let's take a look at some of them.

The Concept of Compound Interest

Albert Einstein referred to it as, "The greatest mathematical discovery of all time". Compound interest transforms your invested capital into a very powerful income-generating mechanism. So what does compounding mean?

It is simply the process of earning interest on the reinvested earnings of an asset. Two things are necessary to make this work; re-investing the earnings and time. If you give your investments more time to grow, then you will make a greater profit. Let me give you a brief example:

If you were to invest $1000 today at 6% interest, you would make $1060 in a year's time ($1000 x 0.06). Instead of withdrawing the $60 interest, let's say you leave it there for another 1 year. Assuming the same interest rate of 6%, your investment will grow to $1123.60 ($1060 x 0.06) by the end of year 2.

When you chose to reinvest the $60 for another year, the interest worked together with the original investment, making $63.60 interest, which is $3.60 more than the previous year. It may not look like much for now, but keep in mind that you did not have to do any work to earn that extra $3.60. Moreover, this $3.60 also has the capacity to generate more interest.

As long as you keep reinvesting your interest, this compounding action will continue.

Getting an Early Start

As an investor who wants to maximize the power of compound interest, you have to realize the power of time. The longer you keep your interest invested, the more money you will make. This means that you are better off starting your investments early in life. These days, people start buying stocks in their teens and twenties, so though there is no right or wrong time, it is advisable to start as early as possible.

It also takes most people a couple of years to get the hang of investing successfully, so make your mistakes while still young, so that you have time to learn from them. Don't wait to get that promotion, perfect job, or reach a certain age. Just start now.

Know Thyself

Before you start wondering about the relevance of this phrase, let me explain. From an investing perspective, success depends on you knowing your personal traits and choosing an investment strategy that fits these characteristics.

There are many investors out there, each with a different background and diverse needs. It makes sense that some investment vehicles are suitable for certain types of investors and not others. Let us take a look at 3 factors that determine the path an investor should take: investment objectives, investor personality, and risk tolerance.

Investment Objectives

As an investor, there are some factors to consider

when you are searching for the best place to put your money. Current income, safety of capital and capital appreciation are factors that affect investment decisions, depending on your age, stage in life and personal situation.

A 70 year old widow will make her decision to cater for value preservation of her retirement portfolio, as she cannot risk losing her investment. A 33 year-old marketing executive can afford to be more aggressive with his investment strategies as he has more time to recover any losses incurred.

A millionaire will not mind risking and losing $100,000 on a real estate investment, but a young newlywed couple trying to save money for a house cannot risk losing money in such a venture.

Personality

What is your personality? Are you a thrill seeker who loves fast cars and risky activities, or do you prefer reading a book in your backyard, enjoying the peace and tranquility?

It is important that you figure out what kind of investor you are before you make an investment decision. How much volatility can you tolerate, and will you spend sleepless nights worrying about your investments? If you cannot stomach the risk, then don't make risky investments.

Risk Tolerance

It should be clear by now that what determines the best investment for you is your capacity to absorb risk. Each individual is different and every investor is exposed to different situations. Bear in mind that an investment is not the same to everyone. If you are unsure, start small and learn as you gradually gain more experience.

Now that you know a thing or two about investing, let us look at some investment vehicles that you can use.

Chapter 2:

Investments Part 1: Bonds, Stocks And Mutual Funds

I have already mentioned some ways of investing your money. One of these ways is to put your money in traditional investment vehicles. Traditional investments are simply investments you put your money in and hold onto.

Even if you want to make some changes in order to protect your capital, traditional investments provide good stability to investment strategies that are riskier or more aggressive. Let us look at these traditional investment vehicles.

Bonds

In order to raise money, governments, governmental agencies, companies, and municipalities may sell bonds.

By buying a bond, what you are doing is lending one of these entities your money with the promise that you will be paid back the original sum plus a specified annual interest.

A bond is simply an IOU that has a serial number. Bonds are also referred to as fixed-income securities and debt securities. So, how can you benefit by investing in bonds?

Pros

Though some entities provide more reliability than others, a bond virtually guarantees you safety, predictability and stability that other investments cannot.

Bonds provide you with a steady flow of annual returns and your principal is also returned at the end of the bond's life.

Cons

Since bonds have little risk, the potential for returns is low. This means that the rate of returns is usually less compared to other types of securities.

Stocks

By buying a company's stocks (or equities), you are essentially becoming part owner of the business. You will be at liberty to attend and vote at shareholder meetings, while also being paid dividends at the end of the year. Dividends are simply the profits a company distributes to its shareholders.

Pros

Stocks have the potential of earning you higher returns than bonds.

Investing in stocks can lead to investment gains as a result of an increase in price of the stock and thus you can sell the stock at higher prices making a profit.

You also get to enjoy dividend income especially from companies that declare dividends

Since you are buying the ownership of the company, you can vote on specific business decisions as well as during annual general meetings.

Cons

Stocks can be quite volatile, meaning they tend to fluctuate every day. This can lead to a decline in stock prices, which will affect the value of your investment.

Unlike bonds, you are not guaranteed anything. Some stocks do not even pay out dividends, so the only way you might make money is *if* the value of the stock appreciates.

There is the risk that you will lose all your money invested in a company's stocks especially if such a

company faces bankruptcy and does not have enough money to pay shareholders their initial investments.

Mutual Funds

By investing in a mutual fund, you are essentially grouping your money with other investors, thus enabling you (and the group) to pay a professional fund manager to pick which securities to invest in. A mutual fund is established with a specific strategy and is able to invest in anything, be it stocks, government bonds, company bonds, or even foreign stocks. So, why invest in mutual funds and not bonds or stocks?

Pros

\# A mutual fund allows you to take advantage of the services of a professional manager. This is beneficial if you do not have the time or the experience required to select a sound investment.

\# Investing in mutual funds provides diversification of your investment in different industries and companies and this greatly spreads your risks.

\# You get to enjoy economies of scale. Pooling of funds from different investors makes it possible for you to invest in greater projects as compared to if you were just alone.

\# Investing in mutual funds is also beneficial because you can easily get in and out of the mutual fund. You can actually sell your mutual funds within a very short time and there would not be much difference between the sale price and the current market value.

Cons

\# Price fluctuations may lead to depreciation of value.

\# Mutual funds are not guaranteed by the US government, so if the fund is dissolved, you lose everything.

\# There are operating and management fees you have to pay, thus reducing your ultimate payout.

Chapter 3:

Investments Part 2: Options, Futures, FOREX, Commodities, Real Estate

So, we have looked at the three fundamental investment vehicles; debt (bonds), equity (stocks), mutual funds. Now it is time to look at other alternatives that represent more complicated investment strategies and securities.

As a first-time investor, it is not advisable to start out by putting your money in these investments. Though they offer the potential for high rewards, these securities are very risky and more speculative than stocks and bonds. They also require you to have some specialized knowledge.

Let's take a look at some of these alternative investments:

Options

An option can be described as a contract that allows the buyer or seller to buy or sell an underlying asset for a given amount, either on or before a specific date. Since options are contracts that deal with underlying assets, they are also known as derivatives. They derive their value from other assets. The underlying assets or securities could be stocks, bonds, real estate investments, products etc.

When you purchase an option, you can choose to do something with it or let it expire. If for instance you buy an option to buy a certain commodity when its price is let's say $100 at a particular date, you can decide to exercise the option before the date if the price is below $100 or you can choose to exercise the option if the market price at the set date is $150.

Most people purchase options to hedge certain risks such as price movements. In the above example, if you did not purchase an option, you would have to buy the particular commodity at a higher value ($150).

Pros

They are versatile in nature. Options enable you to shift your position relative to the situation.

Options give you the opportunity to diversify your portfolio, instead of just sticking to the traditional types of investments.

You can use options to reduce the size of losses, hedging.

Cons

\# Options are a complicated type of security, especially for first time investors.

\# Options tend to be very speculative and risky.

Futures

Futures are a form of derivative instrument or financial contract, where the parties decide to transact either physical commodities or financial instruments at a certain price today, delivered at a future date. Buying a futures contract means you will be agreeing to purchase or sell something at a particular price.

Pros

\# Futures can be used to hedge price movement; thus reducing losses and maximizing gains

\# You can also use futures to speculate the price movement and thus benefit if the price moves in your favor.

Cons

\# Futures contract are standardized contracts drafted at the futures exchange with fixed terms and amounts making it very inflexible.

\# Investing in futures is complex and may not be suitable for first time investors.

Forex

Forex stands for 'Foreign Exchange', which is the financial market where trading of currencies takes place.

If you live in the US and you want to purchase cheese from France, you have to pay for it in Euros. You will have to convert your US dollars into the equivalent value of Euros. This need to change currency is the reason why the Forex market is considered to be the biggest and most liquid market.

This market exists in the online world, i.e. it is conducted electronically through worldwide computer networks. The market is open every hour of every day, five and a half days a week, in almost every country.

Pros

\# Trading in the Forex market is electronic, thus convenient for traders.

\# You can participate in the Forex market from anywhere around the world.

\# You can trade in many different currencies, which are listed in the foreign exchange.

Cons

\# The risks are higher especially since something very small can lead to a currency reducing in value.

\# There are very few trading instruments in the Forex market. There are only eight most traded currencies which combined make for a total of 18 pairs that represent the majority of the trading volume you can trade in.

Commodities

The role of commodities in our daily lives cannot be ignored; whether it is oil, gas, coffee, gold, or oats. Commodities can be traded either in real-time or futures market, though the majority of trades occur in the form of futures.

This means that the value is not in the commodity itself but rather the contract to purchase or sell the commodity at a given price in the future. The key aspect is to buy when low and sell when high.

The trade in commodities has become a popular way for investors to make profits from global demand in grains, meats, energies (crude oil, natural gas) and soft goods (cocoa, sugar, orange juice, etc.).

Pros

\# Commodities are found all over the world, thus can be traded in the world market.

\# The rewards can be great if you are willing to

endure the market swings.

Trading can be done on a very low margin i.e. little initial capital is required.

Cons

The value of the commodities is susceptible to market volatility.

Real Estate

The first thing that comes to mind when we hear about investing in real estate is our homes. Once you buy a house, it becomes part of your investment portfolio.

However, you can invest in several types of real estate investments. You can choose to purchase small apartment buildings, single-family houses, or condominiums for renting out. Unlike stocks and bonds, real estate investments can be seen and touched. It also includes the land the building is constructed on.

Pros

\# Your investment is tangible, creating a pride of ownership, unlike stocks and bonds.

\# Real estate allows you to diversify your portfolio.

\# You can achieve high returns with minimal risk.

Cons

\# It requires you to be more hands-on, unlike trading in stocks and bonds.

\# They are expensive to buy, sell and operate.

\# Real estate market is cyclic in nature – sometimes it's up, sometimes it goes down, depending on demand.

Now that you know the investment vehicles at your disposal, let us see how you can evaluate risk adequately so that you can make suitable investment decisions.

Chapter 4:

How To Properly Evaluate

Your Risk And Returns

There are many stories about people who shy away from the stock market because they fear taking the risk - whether you are a widow afraid of losing your retirement money or a couple who want to buy a new home but fear losing their savings. In most cases, these fears are unfounded and come from a misunderstanding of what risk really means in a financial market.

The few smart people who understand market risks and then adequately assess their ability to tolerate them can turbo-charge their investments. They can accept a certain degree of risk and get rewarded for it.

Understanding Market Risks

Consider the following situation. There are 2 investments. The first one is guaranteed to lose you money – invest $1000, and you will lose $1000. The second investment might offer the opportunity to cash out with $0 to $3000. Which of these investments bears greater risk? Most would point to the first investment because it places their principal in greater jeopardy. However, a financial manager would tell you that the first choice is not risky – but merely stupid – as it is a sure bet that you will lose.

Risk is uncertainty, measured by the degree with which the returns deviate from the norm. You should not measure risk by the chances of loss, but by the variability of returns. Considering the fact that markets have a strong correlation between risk and reward, this distinction can be critical.

In order to understand risk much better, it is important to look at the types of risks that your investment is likely to be exposed to and how to reduce such risks.

Types of Risks

Interest Rate Risk

One of the most common types of risks that you are likely to face when investing is interest rate risk. Interest rate risk is the risk that the value of a security will change because of a change in interest rates. For instance investing in a bond instrument promising 2% interest rate per year can expose you to the likelihood that the particular interest rate can either increase to 4% or even reduce to 1%. So, how do you deal with interest rate risk?

Before making any decision, evaluate the interest rates in the particular bonds that you want to invest or any other investment. If you note that the interest rate is quite volatile and can go either way, you are better of investing in a fixed-rate bond for instance that assures you of a particular fixed income. You can also consider hedging for instance by investing in interest swaps. You can also diversify your investments to cater for the difference in interest rates in different investments.

Credit Risk

This refers to the probability that a bond issuer may be unable to pay the required interest rate payments and the principal repayment. Usually, when the credit risk is higher, the higher the interest rate on the bond. If you are looking to get high returns from bonds, then such bonds are likely to be very risky.

This means that if you want to reduce your credit risk for instance when it comes to investing in bonds you should invest in treasury bills and bonds that may not have such high returns but are usually very low in risk if any.

Inflationary Risk

Inflationary risk also known as inflation risk is the risk that the value of your investment will be eroded as inflation reduces the value of a particular country's currency.

This means that you need to invest in investments that appreciate in value so that the increase in value can cater for the inflation risk and you would still enjoy your investments. Ensure that the growth rate of the investment is always more than the inflation rate in the long term.

Market Risk

Market risk also known as systematic risk and cannot be predicted. This is one of the most difficult kinds of risk to deal with because you cannot simply address market risk by diversification. The only way that you can deal with market risk is to hedge it. You can hedge for instance by using purchasing an option. An option gives you the right to buy or sell a particular good at a certain price in the future.

Let us assume that you want to buy a certain amount of silver six months from now at $1000, you can purchase an option to buy the silver at that price six months from now. If before the six months elapse the same quantity of silver is sold at $800 you can decide to purchase the silver and not exercise the option.

However, if the price of silver after the six months is $1200, you will exercise the option and buy the silver at $1000 saving yourself the $200 had you not entered the option. The only cost you would have to incur is the strike price (price of purchasing the option). So if the strike price was $100 you would have saved $100.

Liquidity Risk

This refers to the possibility that you may not be in a position to buy or sell your investments whenever you want to because of limited opportunities.

When looking at the different types of investment vehicles, I mentioned that mutual funds were very liquid enabling you to sell your investments quickly. Therefore, if you are looking to reduce your liquidity risk, try to invest in mutual funds.

Political/Legislative/Social Risk

These are risks associated with social changes, unfavorable government or passing of unfavorable laws. You can mitigate this risk by investing in not only your home country but also global markets.

It is very unlikely that things will go haywire all over the world.

Exchange Rate Risk

This risk arises from change in price of a currency against another one. The fluctuations in foreign currency can easily affect the value of your investment. You are likely to be faced with this risk especially if you invest in foreign markets. A great way of hedging exchange rate risk is to buy currency swaps. A currency swap involves exchanging principal and interest in a certain currency for the same in another currency.

For example if you are an American who needs to buy sterling pounds and a Briton who wants to buy US dollars, you can arrange to swap currencies by agreeing on an interest rate, amount and maturity date. This will ensure that you are not exposed to exchange rate risk because you will be expecting your investment in US dollars.

Chapter 5:

5 Mistakes Most First-Time Investors Make And How To Avoid Them

Many online discount brokerages provide potential investors with the means to trade in stocks at the click of a button. This easy access to investing is great as people now feel more encouraged to try their hand at investing in the markets, rather than having to depend on fund managers.

However, there are numerous pitfalls that a first time investor has to watch out for, before attempting to choose stocks.

#1 Rushing In Head First

The fundamentals of investing are simple – buy when low and sell when high. However, you have to be aware that what you might consider to be high might be considered low by another investor. In the financial markets, everything depends on different metrics and ratios, so it is quite possible for different conclusions to be made from the same market information.

What you have to do is train yourself to study the basics. You should at least understand some terms such as dividend yield, book value, and price-earnings ratio, while learning how to calculate them and what weaknesses they have. There are online stock simulators that you can use to practice and gain trading skills before delving into the real thing. Sure, the real market is more complex, but at least you will be in a better position to understand what is happening and how to react.

#2 Putting All Your Eggs in One Basket

It is totally unwise to invest all your capital in one specific market, be it commodities, Forex, bonds or the stock market. As a first time investor who does not have adequate know-how of market operations, it is better to diversify and risk small amounts of capital at a time. You may choose to put all your investment in one vehicle once you are familiar with the markets. However, this is still not advisable.

#3 Investing Your Cash Reserves

According to market studies, you will earn a better return on investment if you put your cash into the market in bulk instead of in small increments. However, do not take this to mean that you should invest to the point where you don't have any cash reserves left.

Whether you are a trader or an investor who buys and holds, investing is a long-term game that requires maintaining cash for opportunities and unforeseen emergencies. If all you have is cash to invest with no emergency reserves, then you are probably not ready to seriously invest in the market.

#4 Basing Your Investments on 'News'

Maybe you've heard of a revolutionary new product or a rumor of an investment that offers earth shattering returns, and have decided to base your investments on such information. For a first time investor, this is a really bad move. Sure, you might hit the jackpot and repeat the trick, but the worst case scenario is that you will be investing on a false rumor or putting your money in late.

The best investments for beginners are companies that you are familiar with, as this will make it easier for you to spend time researching that particular investment option.

#5 Investing in Penny Stocks

It may seem like a good idea to invest in cheap, penny stocks. With penny stocks going for as little as $1 per share, you might be tempted to buy more of them instead of blue chip stocks going for $50 per share. An increase of $1 in penny stock share price might double your money, but the volatility associated with them makes them a poor choice.

Penny stocks can go up rapidly, but they can also crash at any time, not to mention their exceptional susceptibility to illiquidity and manipulation. For an investor who is still learning, it is very difficult to obtain any credible kind of information about penny stocks, so steer off penny stocks until you have adequate market knowledge.

Now that you know all you need to know about the basics of investing, let's see how you can go about creating an investment plan.

Chapter 6:

How To Form Your Own Personal Investment Plan And What To Watch Out For

Every investor wants to put himself in a position that will help him succeed. To achieve this goal, it is important that you know your strengths and weaknesses, as well as be willing to commit your time and energy to developing your own personal investment plan.

Let us look at some ways in which you can simplify the often-daunting task of knowing and evaluating your investments.

Evaluate Your Current Position

The first thing you need to do as a first time investor is to make an honest assessment of yourself. You cannot start your journey unless you know where you currently are. In most cases, the younger your age, the more risks you should be willing to take. However, this does not mean that you have to use all your disposable income in investing. If you are an investor under the age of 35, any kind of knowledge you may have about investing is commendable, compared to a majority of people your parent's age.

You should also consider the amount of time the investment will stay untouched, which bears some correlation to your age. If you have a long time horizon of, say, 25 years, you can afford to take some calculated risks comfortably. I don't mean that you jump head first into risky ventures, but you are in a position to participate fully in the equity market without fear of losing substantial sums of your money.

Assess your knowledge of investments by asking yourself some critical questions. You should have some knowledge on fundamental analysis of stock performance; understand the fundamentals of asset allocation, and fixed-income products and how they work. If you do not know any of these things, just create a general asset allocation suitable for your age and simply start off by investing in a few funds.

Be Aware of What You Own

As much as it's important to know your current position, you must also know what you have. Begin by studying your recent financial statements in order to determine the percentage of cash, bonds and stocks you have. You then need to make a decision on how much time you can spare for personal investing. Your objective should be a number of hours per week. The higher the number of stocks you have compared to funds, the more time you need to commit.

If for example you come up with 4 to 5 hours per week, you can settle for owning a few individual stocks. Remember, the time required per stock is not set in stone. It is dependent on your experience and knowledge of the financial markets, so be flexible with it as time goes by.

Evaluate Your Sources of Information

Conducting stock analysis does not require you to subscribe to expensive data services. You can use the internet to look for press releases, earning reports, balance statements, or SEC (Securities and Exchange Commission) reports. Look for trusted sites that present the information in an understandable format, and create links for easier access.

If the website is indeed reputable, it should state its sources clearly and how often it updates the data. This will allow you to feel confident about using their information, as it is likely to be accurate and current.

When performing due diligence on stocks, make sure you set some minimum guidelines in order to streamline the huge amount of information out there. You can filter the thousands of stocks out there by setting valuation caps and minimum market caps.

Develop a Strategy

You can benefit immensely by creating a base asset allocation with ETFs (exchange traded funds) or mutual funds. All you have to do is pick the area of the market that you find most interesting, be it an industry or asset class (bonds, commodities, etc.) and slowly gain the experience necessary to manage your portfolio.

For example, you may be interested in purchasing some technology or healthcare stocks, which together make up 35% of the market share. You should therefore develop a portfolio that allocates 30 – 35% for investing in stocks in those two sectors. You can use the rest of the portfolio for ETFs in other sectors.

It is also recommended that you have a 'watch list' of stocks that you are interested in and have done some research on. You should review this list every week to keep up with any significant changes in the market. By the time you decide to sell some of your stocks in your portfolio, you will have suitable replacements ready in your list.

Re-evaluate and Adjust Your Strategy

Make a timetable for evaluating your progress. It is not about comparing how your investments are doing, but more about reviewing your learning progress and general asset allocation.

Assess the fundamentals to ensure that there have been no significant changes to your portfolio, e.g. the ratio of stocks to bonds. Increase your holding if you feel you must, but remember that this will mean your hourly commitments increase.

Enjoy Your Financial Journey

One crucial thing to understand is that investing is not just about the money. As a first time investor, you are learning, and that is the most important thing. There are so many things to learn about that you simply cannot cover within a 6 month or 1 year schedule. Remember; it is the journey, not the destination that counts.

By taking the time to get more knowledge, you will soon realize that you are making major steps in understanding financial matters. If you feel you know enough about a certain asset class, you can branch out to other types of investments and learn about them too. The greatest dividend comes from taking the time to learn more about investing no matter what type of investment it is.

Conclusion

We have looked at investments, what they are, the basic concepts involved, strategies you can use, and the different investment vehicles available to you. Together, all these points should help you establish a stable foundation of knowledge for comfortable investing.

However, having the concepts and not putting them into practice is useless. You must take the time to learn as much as you can and then use the knowledge to make smart choices.

Take note of the common mistakes most beginners make when investing. You do not want to find yourself penniless and in deep trouble. Remember, create a plan that suits you personally, and use it to guide your investment strategy.

I will be more than happy to learn how this book has helped you in some way. If you feel you have learned something or you think it offered you some value, please take a moment to leave an honest review on Amazon. It would help many future readers who will be forever grateful to you. As I will!

To Your Success,
Adam Richards